Ritual Ob

An Iconography o...

Acknowledgment

In the time immemorial, when the Hindu religious epic Veda was written, the several kinds of artefacts, symbols, emblems also composed by the author with its special significance which are still in force. There are numerous artefacts extracted from the natural substances, artificial objects, musical instruments, weapons etc. which have defined with particular meaning and power.

Tantric Buddhists use specially vajra, of which has several meanings however its most significant meaning is tantrism. Bell and Vajra are used together which signify wisdom and method. In such a way, whatever artefacts are described in this book, these all have particular meanings. Both Hindu and Buddhist use such artefacts in the religious and ritual performance. Uses of such ritual artefacts has glamoured the culture of the eastern religions.

The Artworks and the text has been taken from the several sources of which name has been mentioned in the bibliography for which courtesy the compiler is very much grateful to the previous writers. If any mistakes is found in the book that is due to me which I confes heartily.

Preface

The Yogi Artist is pleased to introduce the significant and comprehensive collection of different types of Hindu and Buddhist ideologies and each of them reflects unique meaning.

The illustration in this book are derived from an ancient art from called 'THANKA' which has been practiced in the Himalayan regions of Nepal.

We, Yogi Artist, have tried to present the symbolism in an integral part of spiritual meanings behind each art work and short description with it. We hope it will be great source in enlightening knowledge of objects.

We, Yogi Artist, are grateful to Venerable Khenpo Phuntsok Thupten Kalsang (Tika), Dinesh Kandel (Ravi), Bidur, Tashi W. Ghale, & P.T. Lama for helping us in various aspects.

Thank you!

Mukhiya N. Lama & Mingyur T. Lama
The Yogi Artists

Table of Contents

AGNI (Fire) མེ།

Used as weapon of war, signifies sacrificial offering, usually carried by Shiva according to Hindu faith. It is common to Hindu as well as Tantric Buddhist. It may be held by the fire god *'Agni'* or may produce from his body.

May

ANKUSH (Hook) ལྕགས་ཀྱུ།

Made of small wooden or metal handle with a strong and sharp hook, It is used by many tantric deities also called Vajrankush when the God is surmounted by Vajra.

Chakyu

AKSHAMALA (Rosery) འཕྲེང་བ།

A symbol of endless cycle of rebirth. It is a string of beads of several kinds which may be made up of seed of dried fruit or other material such as crystal. It is also known as a symbol of Avalokiteshwor in Buddhist tradition. It is used in necromancy, meditation & prayer.

Thengwa

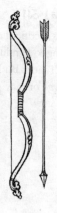

BANA (Arrow) མདའ།

A symbol of consciousness manifested by Tantric deities such as Marichi and kurukula.

Da

BEENA (Lute) སྒྲ་སྙན།

One stringed musical instrument seen in the hand of Goddess Saraswati known as Goddess of wisdom learning and arts. It is also seen in the hand of Buddhist deity Gandharva who is called Diza in Lamaism which is one of the guardian deities of the east direction.

Dangyen

BELL (Ghanta) དྲིལ་བུ།

It is considered to be a female symbol which symbolizes wisdom and purpose. The symbol leads to enlightenment in Tibetan rituals the bell is held in the left hand that signifies wisdom.

Dilbu

CHAITYA (Stupa) མཆོད་རྟེན།

Its shape and size differs - round or square. The stair & steps represents the world of the Gods. The uppermost part of the chaitya whose size is almost seen like triangular shape is the Sumeru mount. Sumeru Mountain, a mythological place where Bodhichitta loses in the Voidness. The four Dhyani Buddhas situates at the four directions, Vairochana one of the five Dhyani Buddhas is situated in the centre of the Chaitya.

Chhorten

CHAKRA (Wheel) འཁོར་ལོ།

Wheel symbolizes the perfectness in the Buddhism. It signifies the wheel of law which turns twelve times or three revolution for each of the four noble truths. It also signifies the occult power of Krishna and Vishnu in Hinduism.

Khorlo

CHANDRA (Moon) ཟླ་བ།

Chandra represents the altruistic intend for the Buddhahood. In Vajrayan Buddhism symbolises a complementary of opposites. It is often seen on the head of the tantric dieties.

Dawa

CHHATRA *(Parasol)* གདུགས།

Chhatra is a symbol of good luck according to Buddhist tradition. It also signifies the goddess Ukhnikha who protests the human beings from the evils.

Dook

CHAMARU *(Fly whisk)* རྔ་མ།

It is one of the symbol of good luck which is held by Hindu deities. It also signifies purification of environment while waging.

Ngama

CHAMCHA *(Spoon)* ཐུར་མ།

The spoon is used to pour *pure* butter in the sacrificial fire. Therefore in the hand of a god, it shows that a god can also sacrifices. This attribute is particularly depicted with Brahma, Sarswati and Annapurna, the general manifestation of Parvati.

Gangza

DIPA (Lamp) མཆོད་མེ།

Dipa symbolizes the human mind. As the light of the lamp has to be the human mind, the Dipa offered to Gods & Goddesses at the ritual ceremony for this purpose but not for paying respect to the divine.

Marmey

DAMARU (Drum) ཌ་མ་རུ།

Damaru is used by both Hindu & Tibetan Buddhist. Specially Tantric Buddhist monk used the Damaru having made of human half skulls as its body. In the Shiva cults, the Damaru associates with the Trident. Most of the monks of higher qualification use only Bell & Damaru at the ritual performance.

Damaru

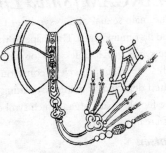

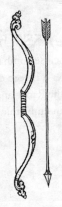

DHANUSA (Bow) མདའ།

Dhanusha associates with the arrow. It has specific meaning as vajra & ghanta like wisdom and method. The arrow represents the power of love where as bow symbolizes the death wish.

Dashyu

5

DHWAJA *(Banner)* རྒྱལ་མཚན།

Dhwaja signifies the Victory for religious affairs.

Gyaltshen

LINGAM *(Shiva Linga)* ཡེ་ག།

The male sexual organ, symbol of the God Shiva and his omnipotence. The shape of the Linga signifies the symbol of formlessness or sunya of the nature. This represents the clear consciousness too. It is often depicted or made associating with the Yoni, the female sexual organ which symbolises the origin of creation.

Fotsen

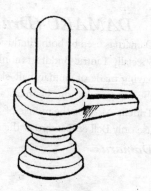

GADA *(Mace)* དབྱུག་ཏོ།

Gada is used as a weapon for close combat. This is the symbol of vishnu. However it is seen carried by Kali, Durga and Bhairava. In the Ramayana this has been used by Hanumana as an emblemic manner.

Yugto

KANGLING (Thigbone) ཀང་གླིང་།

The kangling is the Tibetan word Kanglit ,cans the thigh bone. It is used for driving away the evil spirits through shamanic method. Buddhist Monks aslo largely use this kanglii to chase the spirits. Particularly in Mustang district of Nepal Lama invokes vultures to feed on the dead body by blowing kangling.

Kangling

KALASHA (Vase) ཚེ་བུམ།

Kalasha is a long necked vase where holy water contained. The holy water is considered as elixir by drinking which a man can be immortal. But as a Buddhist faith this water purifies the kleshas of the human mind and it is one of the auspicious symbol among the astamangals.

Tsebum

KARTIKA ཕུགས་གྲི།

It is a weapon wielded by Mahakala symbolizing the severance of worldly bonds by the Dakinis embracing the yidams such as Yama and Yamantaka.

Chagyu

KHADGA *(Sword)* རལ་གྲི།

The Khadga, which is the symbol of Manjushree Boddisattva. It signifies the wisdom or Prajna. This sword destroys the darknes of ignorance issuing out the flame of wisdom. This can be viewed in the picture of Manjushree.

Raldi

KHARTWANGA ཁྱུང་ཏེ་ཤ།

A kind of Tantric club made of human leg or forearm which held by tantric dieties. At the top of the Khatwanga the human skull is necessary to be kept where Vajra also is associated.

Changteu

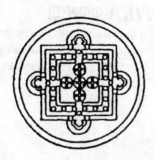

MANDALA མཎྜལ།

Mandala is used specially for the method of meditation which culminates the insight forces for attaining siddhi, This practice exercised by the tantric saints. The graph designed within the square represents various obstacles of impurities which has to cleansed to reach at the innermost part where lotus palace is. The lotus palace represents ultimate attainment.

Kyilkhor

8

MATSHYA (Fish) ཉ

According to Hindu faith the matshya is an incarnation of lord Vishnu. Matshya is associated everywhere with Vishmis icon. In the Buddhism too, Matshya is regarded as one of the auspicious signs among eight.

Nya

MAYURPICCHA
(Feather of peacock) མ་བྱ་སྒྲོ།

The Mayurpichha specially used by Buddhist priest. The kalasa (Bumba) where holy water contained sprinkles that with the help of this mayurpichha.

Shyogdo

NAGA (Snakes) ཀླུ

Naga is regarded as a god of ornament by both Hindu and Buddhist. It is worshipped for the raining also who held the power to bring it. Three, five or seven headed snakes often serve as a protective god's head.

Lu

NAKULA *(Mongoose)* ནེའུ་ལེ།

Nakula is a receptacle of the wealth pressing which the jewels may be vomitted. Therefore the Jambala(Kubera) the god of wealth is associated with the Nakula.

Nehule

PADMA *(Lotus)* པདྨ།

Padma has a descent meaning in the Buddhist tradition which signifies the absolute purity. The God or Demigod stood on the lotus represents that away or above from the cyclic existence. They are abstained from the worldly confusion or muddiness like anger, proud, craving, jealous and sexual attachment. Lotus is regarded as a holy flower for it being a pedal rest of the bodhisatwa.

Pema

NILOTPALA *(White lotus)* པད་དཀར།

It is the symbol of Manjushre and Tara. Nilotpala signifies purity of mind. While the Avalokiteswar holds the lotus Nilotpala called Padmapani.

Pekar

UTPALA ཨུཏྤལ།

This is the half open lotus flower, which stands for the night lotus. It is female principle according to tantric Buddhism. It symbolizes the self creation as "swayamblid'.

Uutpala

PINK LOTUS པདྨ།

The Pink lotus often can be seen in the Thangka. It signifies the sun in Tibetan Buddhism.

Pema

PHURBA (Kila) ཕུར་པ།

An instrument having triangular pointed shape used in vajrayana Buddhism as a weapon killing the effigy of the enemy. It is specially used in ritual performance.

Phurba

MANI (Prayer wheel) མ་ཎི།

It is very common scenario among Tibetan Buddhism that every old aged people hold the prayer wheel. The manual prayer wheel differentiates in shape and size according to users playing capacity. Speciality of this prayer wheel is the mantra "Om mani Padme Hum" which means there is a jewel in the lotus. This type of prayer wheels are installed around the stupa and Monasteries. It is believed that, while muttering this Mantra salvation or Liberation of human being will be ensured.

Mani

MRIGA (Antelope)

As a vedic faith the antelope is considered a powerful animal and its skin is very much important for the ritual performance. It is said that the figure of antelope is depicted at the tip of Shiva!s left hand finger as it signifies that he is the lord of nature.

Shyawa

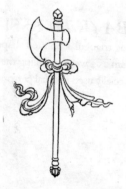

PARASHU (Axe) སྟ་རེ།

Axe is a weapon for overcoming darkness and ignorance as to liberate the people from the web of worldy illusions.

Tari

BHIKSHAPATRA
(Begging bowl) ཕྱུང་བཞེད།

Begging bowl is made up of wooden or metal material or the human skull. That who held human skull begging bowl might be the person possessed shamanic or necromantic power. Otherwise, generally the ascetics carry it for keeping their alms.

Lhungsye

SHANKHA *(Conch shell)* དུང་།

Sankha is used in both ritual ceremony of Hindu and Buddhist. Blowing sankha invokes auspicious moment but it blows at the funeral rites too. The people's faith is different regarding Sankha according to their concept.

Doong

PRASAD *(Manna)* ཚོགས།

In the both religious tradition the offerings of food or fruits are common. Specially it is more prevalent in the lama tradition. It is believed while this fruit or other food stuff offered to the god reciting methodic prayer automatically the blessing of the God strewn on this prashad which the devotees partake and be blessed.

Tshog

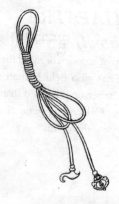

LASSO (Pasha) ཞགས་པ།

The lasso is an attachment to worldly cravings as well as the capacity of the god concerned capturing evil powers. Mostly vajrayani Buddhist wears such a silk and colourful lasso to capture the evil spirits.

Tshedung

KHATKON (Hexagon) ཚོས་འབྱུང་།

Hexagon diagram is common for Hindu and Buddhist as well. Buddhists use this hexagonal chart for astrological purpose but this signifies the union of bi-gendral principles too.

Tshoi jyung-the-nga

SWASTIKA གཡུང་དྲུང་།

As the Buddhist believed that the sign of swastika represents 80 minor marks of Buddha. This kind of mark had been seen in the sole of the Buddha's foot. It also represents the esoteric teachings of the Buddha.

Yungdung

VAJRA *(Thunderbolt)* ཪྡྷོ་ཪྗེ།

Vajra is the symbol of esoteric doctrine of the Bu
dha. Tantric philosophy carried the symbol of vajra.
Although the Hindu proclaimed that Vajra is the
weapon of vishnu, later on Buddhism adopted it.
Vajra signifies several meanings such as the
adamantine doctrine, Diamond sceptor, voidness,
enlightenment etc. Anyway vajra represents tantrism.

Dorjey

VISHWAVAJRA (Crossthunderbolt) ཪྡྷོ་ཪྗེ་རྒྱ་གྲམ།

Double thunderbolt represents the omnipresence.
Tibetan Buddhists believe it as an undestructible
and the wheel of good law. According to Tantra
doctrine it is an emptiness of void which cannot be
cut or destroyed.

Dorjey-gyadam

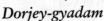

DHOWJA *(Prayer Flag)* ཪར་ཚོག

The identity of the Tibetan Buddhist is the prayer
flags. Wherever prayer flags are fluttered could be
known that the Tibetan Buddhist establishments.
The prayer flag has five colours Blue, white, red,
yellow and green which have significant meanings
as such blue represents sky, white cloud, red
atmosphere, yellow sun and green earth respectively.
Sometimes this emphasizes on one colour, specially
on the funeral rites or religious rites. Along the side
of this flag attached five pieces of similar colour
clothe which manifest the five Dhyani Buddhas.

Dharchyok

15

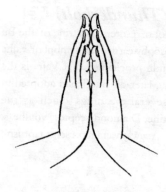

PRANAM ཕྱག

This is a symbol of greeting. One can make pranam on meeting to each other which represents respect as well. Though pranam specifies the spiritual obesience. Good Morning, Namaskar, Tashi Delek or Ohayo Gojaimasu are the same kind.

Chhyag

MONK'S ROBES བླ་ཆོས།

The robes of the monks generally is yellow or maroon colour which signifies renuciation of worldly life. Tibetan monks of some kind of sect use white robes also who is called Tantric monk.

Choe Goe

ADARSHA (*Mirror*) མེ་ལོང་།

Mirror symbolizes a special meaning in the Tibetan Buddhism which signifies the voidness of the world. At the funeral rites, the priest shows the mirror reciting text to the soul of the deceased person to comprehend the emptiness of the worldly substances.

Melong

THANGKA ཐང་ཀ།

Thangka is a written figure of Buddha or Bodhisattva. It is originated in Tibet about 8th century. On the basis of the text, thangka is painted by the monks. Nowadays besides the monks, other laymen have possessed this profession. Thangka is painted in a canvas cloth mixing various Pigments. Some thangkas are depicted with gold and silver price of which is supposed to be expensive than others.

Thangka

KHADA (Scarf) དར་དཀར།

It is a symbol of respect but it is used in various aspects such as for the use of talisman. One who goes for journey offer khada for his protective traveling. It represents welcome as well as offering. The khada is offered enclosing certain amour of money in order to see the higher designated Buddhist monk.

Daar

MAKUTA (Crown) ཅོད་པ་ཅེ།

It is used by Vajrayani Priest during the religious rites. It is made of simple ractangular pentagonal or circle shaped hard paper or cloth where five Dhyani Buddhas figure has been depicted. Tibetan monks do not use this Mokuta the pentagonal shaped Makuta which is called sangay Rigna in tibetan use only for the deceased person before cremation. While performing the religious rites Lama put on long headed ca. which is called Ugyen Peshyo

Chopen.

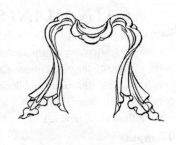

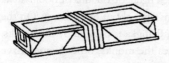

PUSTAK (Book) དེབ།

The pustak is a religious book which called in Tibetan "chhoi". This is a receptacle of spiritual knowledge and the teaching of the Buddha as well as religious and the ritual lessons. It is very much revered by the devotees. According to Buddhist tradition such a book rests on lotus flower as depicted in the picture.

Legbam

RATNAMANI ཕྲེང་བ།

Ratnamani is a rosary of jewels. It represents that it fulfils the intention of the devotee or desirous person. Some of the priest forecast about the future events counting this rosary and declare the patient's condition too. Every devotee holds this rosary for making their mind purified.

Thengwa

TRIRATNA (Three jewels) དཀོན་མཆོག་གསུམ།

This signifies the three basic importance of Buddha, Dharma and Sangha. There Three jewels symbolizes that who go for refuge to Buddha has to adopt with entire motivation.

Norbu

18

KAPALPATRA ग|ष|ल| (ॅिंद|ष|)

A begging bowl which is made of human skull is called KAPALPATRA. The term "kapal" stands for the human skull and the "PATRA" represents a bowl. Specially such a kapalapatra used by tannic monk. Mostly meat and blood is kept within it. The wrathful deity Heruka held such a bowl with full of blood.

Thoipa

KHETAKA ख|बह्ग|ष|

A shield, which is not to be used in the battle but it used as a ritual artifact symbolising to protect the Dharma from evils.

Khetaka

DANDI इ्छग|ष|

This is unlike khatvanga, used as a scepter. It is made of human bone decorated with a skull and the jewels having knob. It symbolises dominance.

Yookpa

KHAKKARA ཁ་དགར།

It is like a scepter in shape but rattles at the top end used by monks signifying their presence or arrival.
Khakkara

VANASPATI བག

Vanaspati represents a mask used to hide real and presents illusion through in fact the manifestation of the divine. The prevalence of such mask is both Hindu and Buddhist. The Buddhist monks celebrate dancing ceremonies using such vanaspati in the festival of "Mani Rimdu" "Bakpa" "Jungba" "Lokhor Chunyo" etc. Such festivals often elevates towards himalayan region. The significance of vanaspati is to terrify the demon that who obstructs in the Dharms.

Baag

GAU གའུ།

A small altar which is carried by the person within what own guardian deity (Istadev) is kept. It is carried everywhere, wherever they go. It is used in the religions, cultural procession too. It is believed that guardian deity protects from the calamity and fulfils the objectives. It is made of metal and decorated in the facade and remained open for seeing the deity.
Gau

SUKUNDA སྦུམ་པ།

Sukunda is a very common ritual artifact used widely in the cultural ceremony. Its shape and size is almost similar to Kalasa, which contains oil for lighting lamp. This symbolises the auspicious occasion to be welcomed.

Bumba-chho-dong-chen

BUMBA ཚེ་བུམ།

This is a water jug. As a ritual object it serves as a sacrificial jug. It usually has no handle but is rather richly decorated with precious stones and metal. Also known as Kamandalu, it is used in pouring water or nectar on the hands of a deity to whom sacrifice is offered. Nectar is the elixir of the immortality and water is the source of life. Among the Hindus and Buddhists it is regarded as an important ritual artifact and is always placed on the altar.

Tsebum

ASTAMANGALA
བཀྲ་ཤིས་རྟགས་བརྒྱད།

The astamangala are attributes of astamangaladevi the goddess of good fortune. Hindus called it Laxmi who is known as goddess of wealth. Astamangala means eight auspicious which is represented by eight kinds of pictures often can be seen depicted towards the house wall, temple, monastery and some other public places.

Tashi tagey

SHRIVATSA དཔལ་བེའུ།

This is an endless knot. It symbolises the endless life circle and eternal love.

Palbiew

DHARMACHAKRA འཁོར་ལོ།

This is the Buddhist wheel of the doctrine of which eight spokess represents the eight fold noble paths. Eightfold noble path is the only method of ever salvation. This wheel has been inscribed in the currency of India or Ashok stambha.

Khorlo

PURNAKALASHA བུམ་པ།

This is a vessel with all the eight signs of good fortune. It represents abundance of auspicity. It is kept on the alter.

Bumba

22

SEVEN OFFERING BOWLS
མཆོད་པའི་ཕྲེང་བདུན།

It is very common that everyone can see the seven offering bowls placed on the alter in every monastery or "chhoisam'. It is quite significant that these seven water offering bowls represent seven limbs of the human body. Seven limbs stand for seven organs. Man should be practised in purifying negative tendencies and accumulate merits. Placing of these bowls should not touch each other, if touched it augurs mentally dull and at the time pouring water into the bowl one should not speak to keep aloof from defilement. Overflowing the rims top is believed to result in ethical detriment and too low level of water augurs a decline in prosperity.

Apart from this, the second significance of these seven bowls it follows respectively that first one represent drinking and rinsing mouth, second washing the feet, third fresh flowers representing the custom of presenting a holy guest with a flower garland and a female guest with flowers for her adornment. The fourth bowl of lamp represents the illumination of wisdom, the sixth bowl contains rose water for refreshing the face and breast and the seventh bowl contains delicious food for the honoured guests. These are known in Tibetan language as Chhoyon, Syabsel, Metog, Dugpo, Marmey, Dichhyap, Syalsey and Rolmo. Here Rolmo is represented by a small cymbal placed beside the Syalsey.

Tshoi-bhe-zedun
Chhoyon, Syabsel, Metog, Dugpoi, Marmey, Dichhyap, Syalsey

MUSICAL INSTRUMENTS རྣ་སྙན།

There are several musical instruments used in the ritual performance in the Tibetan Buddhism among some of them are described as follows:-

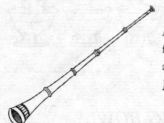

RA-DUNG OR DUNG CHHEN རྭ་དུང་།

A long shaped blowing designed instrument around five to seven feet long played with pair having loud and coarse sound.

Radoong

NGA ཪྔ།

There are two kinds of drums or "Nga' named Lag Naga (Hand drum) used in procession. This is small portable drum. It has a long decorated wooden handle tipped with a Vajra, sometimes somewhat devotees hang silk scarf on the hanging hook tip as a reverence considering God's musical instrument. The wooden handle decoration made the picture of lotus petal upwards and downwards. The drum stick is sickle shaped covered with cloth pad on the tip.

NGA CHHEN ཪྔ་ཆེན།

The double sided drum is called Nga Chhen or big drum. It is more than three feet in diameter hung in the wooden frame. The striker is same shaped for all drums.

Nga-chhen

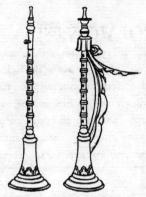

GYALING བརྒྱ་གླིང་།

This trumpet is like western recorder but its tip has bell shaped. Its bone is made of hardwood such as teak or rosewood. The bore rounded by several ring like metal on which precious stone is patched. It has eight holes but used only even with the first underneath. It is blown continiously without breaking sound intermittanly. On the ritual performance or religious ritual performance or religious rites it is blown by the monks till half an hour.

Gyaling

KANGDOONG རྐང་དུང་།

Kangdoong also is one of the Kangling like instrument used for worshipping of peaceful deities. It is made of copper and wooden decorated highly with gilded. While welcome chapter is recited, the all musical instruments are played with loud sound to regard a rival homage.

Kangdoong

SIL-NYAN སིལ་སྙན་།

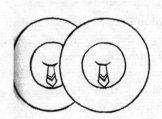

A cymball like instrument having aloes central boss played vertically and used in the rites of peaceful deities.

Sil-Nyan

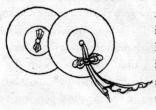

ROLMO རོལ་མོ།

A bit large high domed cymbal is called Rolmo. Used in the rites of wrathful deities but in the lack of Sil Nnyan, this is also used for both purpose. Central issued cloth handles is used clashing, rolling, rotating and muting techniques. Cymbal and drum are played together in the same manner to accompany vocal chanting in the end of the verse recitation.
Rolmo

KANGLING (Thighbone) ཀང་གླིང་།

The kangling is the Tibetan word Kanglit ,cans the thigh bone. It is used for driving away the evil spirits through shamanic method Buddhist Monks also largely use this kangling to chase the spirits. Particularly in Mustai district of Nepal Lama invokes vultures 1 feed on the dead body by blowing kanglin
Kangling

THE PRECIOUS WHEEL
Khorlo Rinpochey འཁོར་ལོ་རིན་པོ་ཆེ།

Chakra, a wheel of dharma which had presented to Sakyamuni Buddha by Brahma (treater) immediately after he attained enlightenment. The golden wheel having thousand spokes symbolizes the thousand dharma or thousand Buddhas of the present era (Bhadrakalpa). Yet pictorially the wheel is usually depicted as an eight spoked wheel representing the eight directions and the noble eight path which the Buddha set in motion.

THE CHAKRAVARTI AND HIS SEVEN PRECIOUS POSESSIONS

འཁོར་ལོས་སྒྱུར་བའི་རྒྱལ་པོ།

Khorlo Gyurpe Longchyod

The term "CHAKRAVARTI" is generally understood as "Universal Emperor" and literally means "Wheel turner" that travels everywhere without obstruction. The prefix "Chakra" represents various meanings as sun, chariot, seven days of the week, emblem of Vishnu, a certain measure of land etc. The turning of the wheel symbolizes both secular and religious authority, it denotes change, movement, extension, conquest and the formation of the new ethical and moral order. It is thus Siddhartha called chakravarti that he possessed seven precious marks, thirty two major marks and eighty minor marks. These include slightly webbed fingers and toes; retracted sexual organs; a fleshy protuberance on the head; lion like chest; thighs and jaws; soft smooth skin; pliant hands and feet; and a thousand spored wheel mark in the soles of the feet.

THE PRECIOUS JEWEL *(Manitara)*

ནོར་བུ་རིན་པོ་ཆེ།

Norbu Rinpochey

The eight faceted precious jewel fulfills all the desires and propensities of the chakravarti and those come around the sphere of its radiance. As stated in the text of Hinduism that a gem named red Kaustube worn by Vishnu and Krishna as a breast ornament would possessed eight magical qualities of the power illuminating the darkness of night. The same kind of jewel having such qualities, it cools when the days are hot and, warms when the days are cold; it causes rain to fall to appear when one is thirsty, it brings to fruition everything that is holder desires. It controls the nagas, preventing floods, hailstorms and torrential rain; it emits various colours lights which heals emotional afflictions; its radiance cures all of the diseases of those who are in its range of healing light; it prevents untimely death, ensuring that death by natural causes occurs in the auspicious sequence of grandfather, father and son. The jewel is described as being smooth, eight faceted, as radiant as the sun, and fashioned of Lupis Lazuli like the Vaidurya jewel. It is often borne on the back of the precious horse, or held in the right hand of the precious minister.

THE PRECIOUS QUEEN (*Striratna*)

བཙུན་མོ་རིན་པོ་ཆེ།

Chunmo Rinpochey

As stated about the preciousness possessed illimitable qualities, the precious queen also described in the same manner. As it to say, precious queen is a most beautiful of all women. Her body has the natural fragrance of camphor, breathing as the scent of the utpala lotus. She possesses thirty two marks of a divine woman, which include long and gentle fingers; a straight and fleshy body; clear bright eyes; eyelashes like the "finest of cows" dark curving eyebrows; pure red lips; forty neatly arranged teeth; a slim soft tongue; beautiful black hair; she has firm and developed breast; soft protruding red nipples; a lotus shaped navel; and a pubic mound like the back of tortoise. She is youthful and lusty, like a sixteen years old virgin. Moreover, she possesses the quality of devotion towards her husband chakravarti, innate feminine wisdom, ever true speaking speech, unjealousy attitude whereas her husband displays amourous behaviour towards other women. Apart from this, she possesses several positive qualities to support her husband to establish the state with peace, prosperity and the happiness.

THE PRECIOUS MINISTER *(Mantriratna)*
བློན་པོ་རིན་པོ་ཆེ།
Lonpo Rinpochey

The precious minister is endowed with the eye of the gods which can see beyond a thousand leagues. Moreover, brilliant, high sensitive, having listening capacity and the great patience which counsel unmistakably to the chakravarti. The minister desires to do only good works to promote the dharma, protecting and benefiting all beings. In the service of his lord, he is able to locate buried treasure to swell royal coffers. In this capacity he is also known as the "Minister" for home economics, a cultured diplomat, he excels at the political affairs of the state, social welfare, religious duties, and ethics, clearly understanding the wishes of the chakravarti. The precious minister often holds wish granting gem or treasury box in his right hand.

THE PRECIOUS HORSE *(Asvaratna)*
རྟ་མཆོག་རིན་པོ་ཆེ།
(Tachhog Rimpochey)

The precious horse bears the thirty two marks of a divine steed. Like the wind horse he travels fast and tirelessly and is capable of encircling the continent of jambudweepa three times in a single day. His body is like a swan and adorned with the golden jewel trappings of the gods. In some traditions he is described as being the blue-black colour of a peacock's neck, with the ability to traverse all of the four continents in an instant. His form is perfect, endowed with a soft mane of ten thousand hairs, and a long flowing tails like a comet. He speedily bears the chakravarti with the royal ease. His tireless moves are silent, light and unflattering. The precious horse often bears the jewels on his saddle, representing the spreading of auspicious blessings throughout the chakravarti realm for wherever the jewels travels it brings all its divine qualities in its wake.

THE PRECIOUS ELEPHANT *(Hastiratna)*

གླང་པོ་རིན་པོ་ཆེ།

Langpo Rinpoche

The precious elephant also possesses the same quality and capacity as such having the strength of ten ordinary elephants, considered as the lord of the bull elephants. It possesses seven limbs- four legs, a trunk and two powerful tusks. The fragrance which exudes from his forehead glands entices all other elephants towards him. As the lord Buddha possessed of sexual organ among thirty two major signs the same quality has in the precious elephant. He is fearless, inexhaustible and assailable with an enduarable capacity at the time of the battle and in the peace time he is wise and dignified. His step is serene and gentle possessing great majesty and beauty. He is perfectly obedient to his master, following his mental directions with perfect telepathic accord. Often he is depicted carrying the precious wheel or the cloth covered alms bowl of sakyamuni Buddha on his back.

THE PRECIOUS GENERAL *(Senapatiratna)*
དམག་དཔོན་རིན་པོ་ཆེ།
Magpon Rinpochey

The precious general wears the armour and helmet of an ancient warrior, forged of metal plates bound together with leather thongs. In his right hand he holds an upraised sword and in his left a shiled, symbolizing his readiness both to wage war and defend the kingdom. His military prowess ensures that he is never defeated in battle, having attained mastery of the sixty four strategic arts of war. His will is attuned to that of the chakravarti, knowing the exact wishes of his ruler. He fights for truth and justice; having abandoned unrightousness acts. He causes no harms to other beings. When the rightousness of dharma has been established throughout the realm, and the peace compassion prevails. The general removes his armour and appears as the "Precious Householder".

33

GZI STONES

རྡོ་གཟི།

Do-Gzi

The bonded and etched agate, known in Tibetan as Gzi stone, is worn as a protective amulet against afflictions of disease, strokes, misfortune, spirit possession and malignant planetary influences. Gzi stones are commonly worn as ornaments around the neck. It classifies in four forms and male and female as well.

THE WHEEL AND DEER EMBLEM

རི་དྭགས་ཆོས་འཁོར།

Ridag Chhoi Kor

The figure of wheel and deer signifies Buddhas first turning of the wheel of Dharma in the Deer Park, Saranath and which occurs one of the main emblems of the Buddhist teachings. This figure is installed on the monastery gate and somewhere on the center roof of the monastery.

STUPA OF THE CONQUEST OF MARA

བདུད་བཅུལ་མཆོད་རྟེན།

Duedul Chhorten

It is designed for commemorating Shakyamuni's defeat of the temptation and attack of the hosts of Mara under the bodhi tree at Bodhgaya, when he was thirty five years old. King Bimbisara is said to have erected a stupa has the traditional unadorned four square steps, often with a slight overhang along the top of the each step.

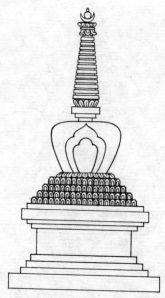

STUPA OF HEAPED LOTUSES
པད་སྤུངས་མཆོད་རྟེན།
Pema pungpe chhorten

This stupa is designed commemorating the Buddhas birth in the royal Lumbini garden on the seventh day of the four lunar month in the year 563 BC. His father, Suddhodhana, is said to have erected a stupa in this design to commemorate this event. At birth Buddha took seven steps in each of the four directions from which lotuses sprang. Symbolising his immediate resolve to embark on the path of the four "immeasurables" The four steps of this stupa are circular and decorated with Lotus petals designs. A tradition also exists of constructing seven heaped lotus steps to represent Buddha's first action. This stupa is also known as the "Lotus Blossom Stupa or the "Birth of the Sugata Stupa!"

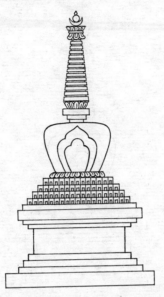

STUPA OF MANY DOORS OR GATES
བཀྲ་ཤིས་སྒོ་མང་མཆོད་རྟེན།
Go mang chhorten

Designed for commemorating the Buddhas first turning of the wheel of Dharma at the deer park in Saranath near Varanasi. His first five mendicant disciples are said to have built a stupa of this design. Each of the four Square steps are decorated with many small door frames which express the many avenues or methods of Buddhas teachings. A series of four, six, eight or twelve doors on each side of the steps symbolizes respectively the four noble truths and the six perfections, the noble eight fold path, and the twelve links in the chain of dependant origination.

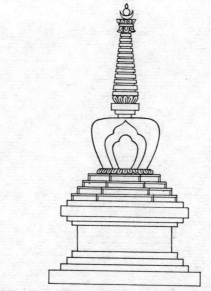

STUPA OF GREAT MIRACLES
ཚོས་འཕྲུལ་མཆོད་རྟེན།
Tsho thul chhorten

Commemorating the Buddhas display of inconceivable miracles in the first half of a lunar month at shravasti, when he was fifty years old. Hear he over powered the Naras and herestics (tirthika) at the jetavana graden. The stupa of miracles or congest of the tirthika's wall was built by the lichhavi tribe to commemorate this event. The stupa of miracles has projecting central section on each of its four steps and sides, which also project slightly by one third of their height.

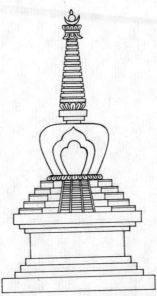

STUPA OF DESCEND FROM THE GOD REALM

ལྷ་བབས་མཆོད་རྟེན།

Lha bab chhorten

It is made commemorating Buddhas descend from the heaven of the thirty three gods (trayastrimsa) when he was forty two years old. He spent the summer retreat in tushita heaven teaching the dharma to the reincarnation of his mother, in order to pay descended at the city of sankashya, and the local inhabitants built a stupa in this design to commemorate the event. The descend from the god realm stupa is characterized by a central projection in each of its four sides containing a triple ladder or project steps "which from a triple ascending ladder were said to have been constructed for the Buddha by the celestial architect Vishwakarma. They often have three rows of thirty three steps symbolizing the god realms laddered stairways in this design are frequently built at temple entrances. The central stairway is reserved exclusively for distinguished or incarnate lamas, the right stairway is for the ordained sangha and the left stairway for lay practitioners. Triple flights of wooden stairs at the potala palace and very worn down on their right and left sides, but completely unworn in their central section as this stairway was only used by the Dalai Lama.

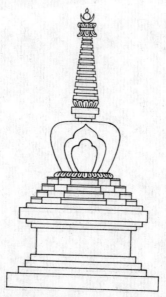

STUPA OF RECONCILIATION
དབྱེན་བཟླུམས་མཆོད་རྟེན།
Indum chhorten

Commemorating Buddhas reconciliation of the deputing factions within the sangha which had been divided by the enmity of his cousin Devadatta. Buddha reunited the sangha at veluvana bamboo grove at Rajgriha, and the local inhabitants of the kingdom of magadha constructed a stupa in this design. The reconciliation stupa is characterized by its four octagonal step with equal sides. Various symbolic meanings are given for the four levels of eight sided steps, which total thirty two in number.

STUPA OF COMPLETE VICTORY
རྣམ་རྒྱལ་མཆོད་རྟེན།
Namgyal chhorten

Commemorating Buddhas prolongation of his lifetime by three months. This event occurred at the city of Vaishali when Buddha was eighty years of age by the supplication of the lay devotee Tsundra. The celestial beings are said to have erected a stupa of this design. The complete victory stupa is characterized by having only three steps which is circular and unadorned.

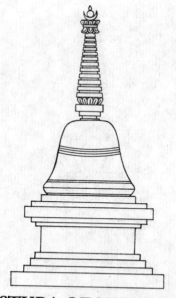

STUPA OF NIRVANA

 སྐུང་འདས་མཆོད་རྟེན།

Nyang de chhorten

Commemorating Buddha passing away 'beyond sorrow' into his final 'parinirvana at kushinagara between two saal trees when he was eighty years old. The malla tribe of kushinagara erected a stupa in this design. The nirvana stupa is characterized by its circular bell shaped dome which rests directly on the circular base of the ten virtues with no ascending steps. Usually this bell-shaped dome is not ornamented, except occasionally when the base or the mouth of the dome is decorated with an ornate ring of inscribed circles. Its simplicity and the absence of steps symbolized the Buddhas complete absorption into parinirvana, there is a touching poignant' in the shape of the dome is an unstrck bell a silent reliquary case, or an upturened alms boes which represent by it inversion the physical death of an enlightened renunciate and his transcended the need for sustenance.

DESIGN OF STUPA
མཆོད་རྟེན་གྱི་དཔེ་རིས།
Thuten Ghishyugtang

Chaitya represents the Buddhist world. Its shape and size differs sometimes round or square. The stair & steps represents the world of the Gods. The uppermost part of the Chaitya whose size is almost seen like triangular shape is the Sumeru mount. Sumeru Mountain, a mythological place where Bodhichitta loses in the Voidness. The four Dhyani Buddhas situates at the four directions, Vairochana one of the five Dhyani Buddhas is situated in the center of the Chaitya.

NAROPA

གྲུབ་ཆེན་ནཱ་རོ་པ།

Maha Siddha Naropa

Naropa, a great tantric scholar, a disciple of Tilopa of whose lineage joins to Tibetan scholars such as, Marpa, Milarepa, Gompopa and so on.

Naropa was the son of a king of then principality of eastern India. He was tended eagerly towards righteous and virtuous attitudes since childhood. He did not want to marry that his parents advised. He intended to move Kashmir for the religious study and there he met a teacher whose name was Namkhai Nyingbo (Akasgarva) who named Naropa, Sai Nyingbo (Kshitigarva) as a consecration. After returning from Kashmir, Naropa was forced again with the marriage proposal by his parents. At this time, he could not retaliate but agreed on some conditions that his parents accepted.

His severe efforts of attaining higher religious education fulfilled meeting a most prominent tantric scholar Tilopa. On the process of looking for Tilopa, he faced several complications and confusions which he passed through unknowingly. When he met Tilopa, then he had wisdom of six kinds of top esoteric teachings which has been still following by Kagyupa order. Naropas life history cannot suffice to mention on a single page.

TANTRIK MASTER

གྲུབ་ཆེན་ཏེ་ལོ་པ།

Tilopa

Once upon a time there was a king in Bengal (9 century AD). His kingdom was like that of Kubera and his palace was decorated with gold, silver and precious gems. He had three sons. Once astrologers were called to find out who will inherit the king to rule the kingdom. The astrologer declared, if the middle son becomes king, the kingdom will flourish, subjects will also be happy. Hearing all other points of good men, the king gave him the responsibility of the kingdom. The elder brother, the younger brother and the kinsmen altogether chained him in gold. He bribed the guard and watchman with gold and silver, dressed as a common man, escaped giving gold as a prize even to the guide. He reached Rameshwar, the kingdom of Ramal.

After that when he went to Bodhgaya, a heavenly Dakini accepted him as a disciple and initiated him. When he went to his own land, Saliputra (Kingdom of old Bengal), he accepted food from anybody and made his home on cremation ground and nobody recognized him. One day in the market, he entered into a wine shop. The head of the bar-tender girl was a secret dakini. Seeing the prince she thought, this person has purified his four chakras but due to a little misconception he is not absolutely clean. Thinking this, the lady served decomposed food in the plate of the prince. Seeing that the prince threw it off. The Dakini said wrathfully - If you cannot be indifferent to good and bad food, what is the meaning of practicing dharma?

Realising that the thought of difference is bar to attaining perfection of wisdom, the prince left it. The entrails of fish that the fisherman used to throw away beside the River Ganga, he used to collect them to live upon. Thus, he meditated for twelve long years. Because he used to eat the entrails of fish called "Lui" in their language, the fisherman's wife used to call him Luipa. The entrails eating Siddha. He became famous as "Luipa' far and near. He became siddha in this name. The time rolled by Luipa word has been slightly changed joining "Ti" as a prefix in the Luipa and is known Tilopa, a certain distorted form of the word Luipa.

MARPA LOTSAWA
མར་པ་ལོ་ཙཱ་བ།
Marpa

Marpa was born in 1012 A.D. in the region of Lhotrak (Lotak). This region is in the extreme south of Tibet, right above the border of Bhutan, it is the region of forests and fertile farmland, of agriculture and grazing flocks and herds. Marpas parents were wealthy landowners, with both farmland in the lowlands and grazing pasture in the high lands. As Marpa was aggressive child, his parents decided to entrust him to dharmic training, lest he become too aggressive and destructive. Thus Marpa began his education at the age of twelve, and received his Buddhist name, Choikyi Lodo (Intellect of Dharma). True to his name, Marpa quickly mastered both reading and writing. Marpa learnt Sanskrit in Nyugu and colloquial language of India. This was the foundation of Marpa of own training as Lotsawa.

Having rolled with several troubles in the verge of looking further education, Marpa arrived in India and met Naropa, a prominent Tantric Scholar of that time. He learnt there many esoteric education of Vajrayana with Noropa. From the first visit to India. While he revisited to India he met his all teachers and had more practical experiences on tantric doctrine, then he became a Master of Vajrayana education of whose prominent disciple is Milarepa, a worldwide famous yogi.

46

MAHAYOGI MILAREPA
རྣལ་འབྱོར་གྱི་དབང་ཕྱུག་ཆེན་པོ་རྗེ་བཙུན་མི་ལ་རས་པ།

Mila

The life of Milarepa (1040-1123) according to his disciple Rechungpa narrated in the Mila Khabum. He was the Yogi of Tibet of all times. As he was not only a mendicant but also a poet and composer of thousand and one songs. Under Marpa, Milarepa studied and was subjected to power discipline, including the labour of building and repeatedly rebuilding the nine-story stone tower of "Shekhar GuthoW'which still stands in Lhodag (Southern Tibet). He preserved, however, in spite of everything, and was also encouraged and sustained by the kindness of Marpas wife Nairatmya, Later Milarepa learnt that in his absence his widowed mother and that family had been enslaved by evil uncle, and he went and took revenge by magical means. After that he turned to the life of wandering yogi, and lived in many solitary places. By Virtue of the inner mystic heat (tummo) he was able to endure the coldest weather in only cotton clothing, hence his familiar name, Milarepa, "The cotton clad Mila', dwelling at Mount Kailash and Lake Manasarovara. The position of seating of Milarepa seems to have been with Lotus Asana. He was short and with curly hair and dressed by simple white cotton cloth wrapping his body. He always holds his right hand with a finger extended and the palm turned outwards behind his right ear, as if is listening the echoes of nature. His left hand holds a begging bowl. Milarepa is regarded on the master of Kagyu-Sect

GAMPOPA
རྗེ་སྒམ་པོ་པ།

Gampopa (1079-1153) was the founder of Kagyu Sect, he who was the disciple of great yogi Milarepa. The accounts of his life and works must have been scattered here and there. Gampopa wrote a book- "The jewel ornaments of liberation' which translated by Herbert V. Guenther in 1959. In his youth age, he studied medicine and became quite a scholar in that science. An early marriage ended tragically by the death of his wife, son and daughter when he was just past twenty due to natural catastrophe. On her death bed, his wife said to him not to remarry, but it is safe to assume that her sudden death made a deep impression him so that he devoted himself to a religious life. Gampopa was a simpler not at all pedantic. He studied through Kadampa tradition and later on practiced Mahamudra a unique manner of tantric Buddhism. He had many disciples and was the organizers of Kagyupa order.

Gampopa deals with the world of Buddhism as a way of life. He is convinced that every sentient being is capable of attaining enlightenment. Especially, Gampopa is known for founding the Kagyupa school of thought. This school could very much be called a revised version of Kadampa which was started by Atisa. This set laid great emphasis on monastic discipline, various steps of meditation and the regulation of the relationship between trantrism and philosophy.

KARMAPA

ཤ་རྒྱལ་བ་ཀརྨ་པ།

In the Tibetan Buddhism, Karma Kagyu Sect is regarded one of the most popular and famous principles. The Kagyu lineage starts from the first Karmapa, Duisum Khenpa.

Prior to mention about Karmapa, it is essential to brief regarding Karma tradition.

The Kagyupas are the "Command lineage" where "Ka" meaning "Speech" refers to the oral instructions of the guru to his pupil, this relationship of the two being of special importance in this order, and described as the relationship of a spiritual father and son. The spiritual lineage of the Kagyupa usually beings with the Adi Buddha (Primordial Buddha) under the name of Vajradhara (Tib, Dorjey Chhang) or sometimes it begins with the Heruka and tutelary deity (Yidam) Chakrasambhara (Tib, Khorlo Demehhog) together with his Dakini (consort) Vajrayogini (Dorgey Phagmo).

Tshurpu monastery, in the eastern Tibet is the main seat of the Karmapa lineage. In 1959, due to the political problems in Tibet, It's holiness the 16th Karmapa Rigpey Dorgey went to Sikkim where he established the chief center of the Karma Kagyu sub order. After passing away the 16th Karmapa, the 17th Karmapa Urgen Thinley has been reincarnated. He has been recognized as Karmapa but the dispute of the dissatisfied party entangled to enthronement.

THE DHARMA KING SRONGTSEN GOMPO
ཆོས་རྒྱལ་སྲོང་བཙན་སྒམ་པོ།

Srongtsen Gampo is known as a founder of Tibetan civilization. He was born on 617 A.D. in the middle part of Tibet named Kongpo. He ascended on throne at the age of 13 after his father's death. But he did not satisfy only with this little state, he collected Tibetan warriors and invaded on central provinces western province Tsang and Gilgit and captured upto Turkisthan of the north. He had married the princess of those provinces which he defeated. He made a big state of his own defeating peripheral provinces. It is said that the forefathers of Srongtsen Gampo's were attributed from India named Kosalraj Prasenjit who was five hundred years before Christ.

H.H. *The 14th DALAI LAMA*

༄༅རྒྱལ་དབང་བསྟན་འཛིན་རྒྱ་མཚོ།

The Dalai Lama, an internationally renowned religious leader was born in 1935 in the north eastern ethnic Tibet at the village of Taktser in the district of Amdo was recognized as the reincarnation of 13th Dalai Lama and enthroned at the age of four his name being Tenzing Gyatsho.

The reign of the 14th Dalai Lama saw reforms undertaken in the ancient feudal structure of Tibetan society, but interrupted by Chinese invasion which had been taken place on 1959 and in the very attack on Tibet Dalai Lama took shelter in India along with his hundred thousand people.

The Dalai Lama of Tibet is loved and respected worldwide as a man of peace. As spiritual and political leader of the Tibetan people, he has consistently advocated policy of non-violence, even in the face of great aggression - an approach that in 1989 won him the coveted Novel prize. In lectures and tours around the world he has touched people's hearts, transcending religious, national and political barriers by the simplicity, profoundity and great heartedness of his message that of universal responsibility and great compassion. At present, he has been residing in Dharamsala, India, where the offices of the "Government in Exile" of Tibetans has been established.

51

PENCHEN LAMA
པཎ་ཆེན་རིན་པོ་ཆེ།

In the arena of Tibetan Buddhism there are two heads as such - the political head is Dalai Lama and religious head is Penchen Lama. Both are attributed from Gelukpa order. Dalai Lama looks into the matter of Temporal aspect whereas Penchen rules over the religion. Penchen means "Precious great Scholar" or Mahapandita. The incarnation lineage begins of Penchen Rimpochey from Lopsang choiki Gyentsen. His authoritative position starts only after 1642. In the spiritual realm the Penchen Lama is actually of higher rank than Dalai Lama, for the Penchen Lama is not only the reincarnation of his predecessor but also the incarnation of Amitabha (Hopame). The seat of Penchen Lama is the Tashilhunpo monastery thought both Dalai Lama and Penchen Lama were the abbots of Ganden monastery.

THOUSAND HANDS AVALOKITESWARA

ཕྱག་རས་གཟིགས་ཕྱག་སྟོང་སྤྱན་སྟོང་།

Chenresig Chhyagtong Chentong

Sahasrabhuja Avalokiteswara is a cosmic form of Avalokiteswara. He is represented with eleven head and one thousand arms. The basic image is of the eleven headed and eight armed Lokeswara. The eight arms of Sahasrabhuja has more prominent position and other remaining one are distributed on either side to form a Mandala. These arms are sometimes marked with eyes. The eleven head at the top is that of his parent tathagata, Amitabha. The tenth head is terrifying and all others are placid. The principle pairs of hands is held against the chest in the gesture of adoration while the upper most hands holds the rosary and the full blown lotus. This four hands thus represents the aspect of the Bodhisatva known as Kharcheri. The other four hands display the jewel and the gesture of the charity on the right and the pot and the bow and arrow one the left.

CHAKRASAMBHARA
འཁོར་ལོ་བདེ་མཆོག
Demchog Khorlo

Chakrasambhara is a consolidated form of Tantrik text of Vajrayana Buddhism which has deified in a fierce god. He is also regarded as manifestation of Hayvajra who is the central figure of an esoteric cult of the Vajrayana Buddhism. Vajravarahi is his consort embracing in a mystic position. Their embrace symbolizes ultimate bliss. As stated above, this texts consists of more than 2 lakh 7 hundred verses.

KALACHAKRA

དུས་འཁོར།

Duikhor

Mostly in Vajrayana Buddhism, some texts of Tantra has been deified as charasambhara, Prajna-Paramita and Kalachakra as well. The Kalachakra Tantra takes its name in Tibetan "Dui Kyi Khorld' which is the black wheel of time or of death. Kalachakra also is the name of Yidam of this tantrik system, he is usually seen as a fierce deity and in association with his Dakini. As the name of the deity and of the tantra suggests the system has to do especially with over coming the hazards of time and of death.

ATISA

རྗེ་བོ་རྗེ་དཔལ་ལྡན་ཨ་ཏི་ཤ།

Dipangkar Shrigyan

Atisa

Atisa is known with Dipankar Shrigyan too, who founded a school of kadampa order in Tibet in around 11th century. He was one of the masters of Nalanda University before to move to Tibet. Towards the southern part of Vikramsila Mahavihar a small feudal state was in existence, Atisa was the prince of that state. He did not study only in Nalanda, Vikramsila, Bodhgaya and Ragriha, but he went in the south east country Java, Sumatra also for studying Buddhism. Finalising all his discipleship, he started teaching in Nalanda as being one of the most reverent teachers meanwhile there were eight teachers of the same category at that time.

While he was teaching in Nalanda, an invitation from Tibet, though Ye-Shey-o received eventually which he treated as refusal. Again, in the second time, a princely monk Jyang-chup-o sent some people to Atisa and they referred the dedication of Yeshe-o towards Buddhism; In this time he was convinced and accepted the invitation. From the lake Manasarovar Atisa proceeded to the monastery of Tholing where he wrote a book named "Bodhipathpradipa!". It was the year 1042 when Atisa arrived in Tibet. Atisa remained for some years in western Tibet and proceeded towards central Tibet. Atisa said to his lay disciple Domton to Construct a monastery. Although Domton was not agreed with his instruction but Atisa obliged him and in the long run Domton constructed a monastery where he taught the four noble truth for nine years. Atisa did not return to India to fulfill his promise with Nagtsho one of the teacher of Nalanda.

MANJUSHRI

ཇེ་བཙུན་འཇམ་དཔལ་དབྱངས།

Jampalyang

Manjushri means "Charming splendor" is the Bodhisatva of wisdom and literature, is shown in yellow, white, red and black forms, with two lotus blossoms as his attributes, with the sword (sometimes flaming) of knowledge it his right and the book of transcendent window (Pragya Paramita) in his left hand incarnate in king Thrisong Deushan and in Tsongkhapa.

Manjushri known as "God of Divine wisdom', whose worship confers Mastery of the Dharma, retentive memory, mental perfection and eloquence. In Nepal, he is considered as the founder of Nepalese civilization and the creator of Kathmandu valley. According to the tradition, he was a Chinese saint. He carries the sword of wisdom and light in his right hand and "Prajna Paramita Manuscript". "The book of divine wisdom' on his left the lotus blossom. His left hand will be in preaching gesture. People believe that the worship of Manjushri can confer upon them wisdom, memory, intelligence etc.

PADMASAMBHAVA
སློབ་དཔོན་པདྨ་འབྱུང་གནས།

Guru Rinpoche
Lopon Pema Jyungney

There are various legends about Padma Sambhava who is known as "Guru Rimpochey" also in the Lamaism. It is believed that when Lord Buddha was about to pass into final Nirvana, he said to his followers, this worldly life is transitory and separation is inevitable. A miraculous person who will born in the lotus flower in the immaculately pure lake in the northwest of Uddiyana will appear wiser and more powerful than myself. He will reveal the teachings of the secret mantras to deliver all beings from misery is the incarnation of mine in as esoteric form.

Padmasambhava was the adopted son of the blind king Indrabodhi of Uddiyana, Uddiyana lies in the swat valley in the Northwest of Pakistan. He studied sometime in the Nalanda University and later taught there. According to Pema Kathang (The history of Padma) one of his teachers was Hunkaravajra known as Suratvajra also who attributed to Kathmandu, wotu tole, near Indrachowk.

A legend says that Padmasambhava had a miraculous death. Padmasambhava, according to a legend, did not die when his mission concluded, he left Tibet riding through the clouds on a winged horse.

JE TSONKHAPA (Sumatikriti)

རྗེ་ཙོང་ཁ་པ་བློ་བཟང་གྲགས་པ།

Lobsang Dhakpa

Tsongkhapa was born in the district of Tsongkha, meaning onion Valley. Though his original name was Lodoi Dagpa. He is known with the name of "Je Rimpochhey" or the "Precious ruler" as his name reflects. In the north eastern Tibet, or Amdo district, where Tsongkhapa was born there was Kumburn Monastery. At the very early age he received a consecration from Rolpe Dorgey who was the fourth Gyalwa Karmapa (1340-1383), and as a boy of eight he received a further consecration and an introduction to the disciplinary rules "Vinay" and to the tantra, from a great spiritual friend named Dondup Rinchhen, who also gave him the monastic name Lopsang.

At the age of sixteen Tsongkhapa went to centrol Tibet and for many years studied with famous teachers of Nyingmapa, Sakya-pa, Kagyu-pa, Tshalpa, Phakmotupa, Nyingmapa, Lekyi Dorgey, The sakyapa, Redapa, who was the disciple of the sakyapa teacher Rongchong Rawe Senge and the Kadampa Lamas chhokyap Sangpo and Bumapa, the last two being those who especially introduced him to the tradition derived from Atisha. The Lama Bumapa who was also said to have brought Tsongkhapa into mystic communication with the Bodhisattva Manjushri, to whom Tsongkhapa turned for guidance at various points in his life. Tsongkhapa himself was also regarded as an incarnation of Manjushri, therefore sometimes Tsongkhapa is seen with the symbol of Manjushri but with yellow hat. Tsongkhapa is the founder of Gelukpa sect reforming the new Kadampa tradition.

MEDICINE BUDDHA

སངས་རྒྱས་སྨན་བླ།

Sangey Menlha

Bhaisajya guru is known as medicine Buddha. He is also called the healing Buddha. He is said to dispense spiritual medicine when property worshipped. It is even believed that an efficacious are maybe accomplished by merely touching the image. In Tibet he may be represented either as a Buddha, he has the Urn the four superior marks of a Buddha Ukhnikha (a buldge or protuberance in the skull of the Buddha, the first superior marks of Buddha) short and curly hair. He means a monastic robes, is seated with the legs crossed. His left hand lying in his lapin meditation mudra. Usually hods the medicine either a branch with fruit, or the fruit alone of the myrobalan, as medicinal plant found in India and other

SAMANTABHADRA
མདས་རྒྱས་ཀུན་ཏུ་བཟང་པོ།
Kuntu Sangpo

There are three groups with sixteen (Bodhistvas). Among these three groups, one group is headed by SamantaBhadra (Universal Goddess). So, he is important as the leader of sixteen Budhistvas. He is not less important than the future Buddha Maitreya who is head of the two other lists of Buddhisatvas.

He embraced by his consort "DharmaVajrd' his nackedness symbolizes that non-existence form.

WHITE TARA
ཇེ་བཙུན་སྒྲོལ་དཀར།
Dolkar

The White Tara or "White Saviouress" is to probably the incarnate in Thisum then princess of Nepal. As a legend, White Tara was born from a tear of the Bodhisattva of compassion, Avalokiteswara. She holds a very prominent position in Tibet. As she is being a companion of Avalokiteswara is also considered closely related to the Dalai Lama as himself is incarnation of Avalokiteswara. Tara is believed to protect the human beings while they are crossing the ocean of existence and is worshipped in order to promote and succeed the business.

Among the two forms of Tara, White Tara is regarded as consort of Avalokiteswora, sometimes of vairochana. She is usually portrayed seated, dressed and crowned like Bodhisatvas. And sometimes she is regarded as Saptalochana or Seven eyes Tara. Extra eyes on her forehead, palm, feet and lotus flower at one or both of her shoulder. She is related in Vajra posture, white in colour and peaceable manifestation.

GREEN TARA

ཇེ་བཙུན་སྒྲོལ་ལྗང༌།

Dolma

Green Tara embodies the female wisdom activity of the mind and she is regarded as spiritual consort of Amogasidhi, the Dhyani Buddha. She is portrayed similar to the White Tara. Green Tara holds a half-closed lotus flower in her left hand. Sometimes she holds a water lily flower with long petals. She is also called 'Mother of All Buddhas' and has many peaceful and wrathful emanation forms. Results of the Green Tara meditation are e.g. quick thinking and according wisdom-reaction, generosity, magical perfection, fearlessness and spontaneity to reach a quick karmic completion.

She is adorned with jewels and precious cloth, sitting on a white moon-disk. Her right leg is outside the lotus flower, which symbolizes her continuous activity, alterness and her determination for quick active help. Her hands are in the gesture of granting protection and relief from fears. In the Lamaeist Tradition, Tara is incarnated in all good women. She is also to have mortal base in historic persons of the Nepali and Chinese princess who married the great king Strang-Tsan Gampo and credited with the introduction of Buddhism to Tibet and China. She is worshipped, because she brings all good women. One of the main Tara in this group is Aryatara.

ASANA
གདན།

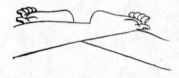

The pose which shows at a glance whether this god is The pose which a god is in a relaxed mood or in an aggressive or contemplative mood. These asanas are defined as yoga too. In the modem age the popularity of the Yoga has been developed. Most of the well to do family, film stars, models and body builders practices the Yoga. It is physiotherapy to build up the body & health.

POSTURE OR GESTURE
ཕྱག་རྒྱ།

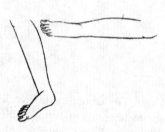

We can see the picture of gods and goddesses depicted in the various gesture and posture. We think it is a style of art designed by the artist itself but it is our wrong concept. On what position the god has depicted this is his manifestation is ferocious, it seems that this deity's duty is to drive away the Mara or evil spirits terrifying them with fearful appearance.

PEDESTAL
ཕྱག་རྒྱ།

Divine feet never place on the earth or ground, it signifies that the divine is not subjected to worldly laws or materialistic illusion. Divine has the certain pedestal or seat. Most of the divines place their feet on the lotus flower or some kind of special pedestal and some are on their vehicles as lion, elephant, swan and horse.

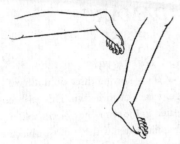

NRITYAMURTIA SANA
ཕྱག་རྒྱ།
Yontsheykil

The Hindu God Natraj position is Nrityamurti Asana. Shiva and some other tantric gods are found in this asana.

GAJA
གླང་པོའི་ཕྱག་རྒྱ།
Langboi-chhyagya

The arm is stretched diagonally across the chest with the fingers pointing down. The gesture symbolizes an elephant's trunk; it is a sign of the greatest strength and power. It is seen above all in Shiva or Natraj.

PATAKA
ཕྱག་རྒྱ།

The legs are stretched like the wing of a bird, symbolizing strength, sometimes this gesture also refers to the power of flames in the fire.

HASTAVASTIKA
ཕྱག་རྒྱ།

The arms crossed in front of the chest indicate total surrender to a god with a superior position.

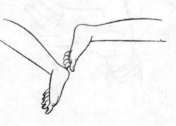

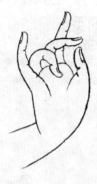

DAMARU
ཌུ་མ་རུ།
Daruigya

This gesture and the following three do not have any symbolic significance of their own. This gestures are so closely related to the symbolic objects holding that they are often illustrated without those objects, assuming the symbolism of the object. Damaru hasta is the gesture with which the damaru is held.

KATAKA
ཕུག་ཀྲ།
Pemai Chayagya

Holding a lotus flower, this position of the hand invites the believer to make the gift of a flower.

ARDHACHANDRA
ཕུག་ཀྲ།
Da chhey chhyagya

This is the gesture with which the god carries fire either with or without a fire dish.

KARTARI
ཕྱག་རྒྱ།
Shyawe chhyagya

Attributes are often held with this gesture. If the gesture is made without an attribute between the outstretched index and middle finger, it symbolizes the antlers of a deer, representing the contradictions inherent in all things.

ABHAYA
མི་འཇིགས་པའི་ཕྱག་རྒྱ།
jigmey

Abhaya mudra signifies the protection for the beings. The arm is elebated and slightly bent as the posture seen like the signal for waiting command. This mudra is the symbol of Amoghasiddhi.

BHUMISPARSA
ས་གནོན་ཕྱག་རྒྱ།
Sanongi Chhyagya

The earth touching with the fingers is called Bhumisparsh mudra. This signifies that the witness, commemorating Gautam Buddhas victory over temptation by the Demon (Mara). This gesture is characteristic of Dhyani Buddha akshobhya as well as Shakyamuni.

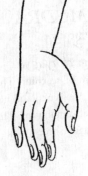

DHARMACHAKRA
ཆོས་འཁོར་ཕྱག་རྒྱ།
Chhoi kor gi chhyagya

Dharmachakra mudra is the gesture of teaching. Dharmachakra represents the law of Dharma. In this gesture both hands are held against the chest. The left facing inward. It is the characteristic of vairochana. While Lord Buddha performed his first sermon had been shown this gesture.

DHYANA MUDRA
མཉམ་གཞག་གི་ཕྱག་རྒྱ།

symbolizes the hands are placed on the left with fingers fully palms faced upwards is placed on it. This is gesture of Amitabha.

JNANA MUDRA
ཡེ་ཤེས་ཕྱག་རྒྱ།
Chhoi jyin gi chhyagya

Jnana mudra is the gesture of teaching. The tip of the index and the thumb are joined and held near the center of that with the palm inward. This is the characteristic Mudra of Manjushree.

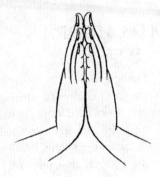

NAMASKAR MUDRA
ཐལ་མོ་སྦྱར་བ།
Chhyag chhal

This mudra symbolizes the characteristics or Avalokiteswara. The hands are joined as offered greetings.

TARJANI MUDRA
ཕྱག་རྒྱ།
Digjub

Tarjani Mudra is the gesture of threatening of warning unless the finger is raised while the other fingers are locked up in the fist. This mudra is characteristics of most of the wrathful deities.

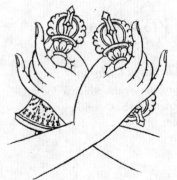

VAJRAHUNKARA MUDRA
ཕྱག་རྒྱ།
Nam nangi Chhyagya

Vajrahunkara Mudra is the gesture of Adi Buddha vajradhara. In this gesture, the wrist are crossed at the breast. The hands hold usually the vajra and ghanta. This is the special mudra of vajradhara and sambhara and most of the gods when holding their saktis.

VARADA MUDRA
Tshog Jyi

Varada Mudra is the gesture of charity or conferring boon or grace. The arm is extended all way down with plan facing outwards, fingers extended downwards, this is the mudra off Dhyani Buddha Ratnasambhava avalokitaswara, sometime, of a Salcyamuni.

VITARKA MUDRA
Tshoi Jyin

Vitarka Mudra is the gesture of argument. In this gesture the tips of thumb and index finger touched forming a circle. All the other fingers are extended upwards. This is the mystic gesture of Taras and Bodhisattvas.

VISMAYA
Khebargi Chhgya

This is the gesture of surprise which a god makes only when he recognizes the superiority of another god who is present.

70

ANJALI

བཕལ་མོ་སློར་བ།

Duibhe Chhyag

The hands are loosely held together with the palms and the fingers stretched up. If they are in this position in front of the chest, this denotes worship. If they are held in front of the forehead, the gesture can also be a greeting.

SWASTIKA

གཡུང་དྲུང་།

Yungdung

Swastika is a Sanskrit word, which means doing good for all. It is very ancient oriental symbol and later on it became an emblem of law. This symbol can be seen in wood-carvings, bronzes, castings, thankas paintings and many other traditional forms of art. The four hand of Swastika signify Friendship, Compassion, Happiness and Indifference. The right hands (clockwise) Swastika represents evaluation and the left hand (anti-clockwise) swastika represents winter sun. Both Hindu and Buddhist worship them equal.

KHATKON

ཚོས་འབྱུང་།

Tshoijung

The Khatkon is composed of two set of triangle. One of the triangles indicates Shiva and the other symbol of Shakti. This popular symbol that indicates the union of the two is widely used on most of Nepali arts such as Mandasla, Windows and other carving and paintings. The Khatkon signifies five basic senses and the extra sensory perception, which significantly makes it the six-pointed star. This symbol is believed to have originated from the Tantric Hinduism.

71

OM (AUM)

ༀ ༀ

Om

OM (AUM mantra; Pranava) is a widely recognized mantra used by Hindu Yogis to represent a vibration which they say pervades the entire universe. They believe this is the same sound as the one heard internally as a result of practicing yoga. More generally, Om represent God, the supreme, all that is. OM is this entire universe. Aum is a variant spelling of Om. The word can be spelled either way because the letter '0' is regarded as a dipthong consisting of 'A' and 'U'.

According to one of the most famous Hindu scriptures, the Mandukya Upanishad, Om symbolizes the four states of consciousness. The letter 'A' represents the waking state, U represents the dream state, 'M' represents deep sleep, and the whole word represents the fourth state which is the state of enlightenment.

SHIVA LINGAM

དབང་ཕྱུག་ལི་ཧྒ།

Wangchhukki Linga

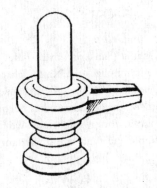

The Lingam is the phallic symbol generally identified analogue of cosmic deity. It occupies the "womb cell" in temples while the outer structure of this double sex deity signifies its determined creative function or creation. In Tantra it is described as sexual self-relation. It is Pre-Vedic.

Apparently the Lingam originally stood for the formlessness of the nature, later for clear consequences and much later for Shiva, the masculine energy.

SHANKHA

དུང་།

Doong

Shankha is Sanskrit word used to donate a sleek and smooth conch shell. It is believed that if the Shankha is blown with skill it can scare away evil spirits and described as a killer of germs and enemies. According to some scholars, it can also be used for preparing many kind of aurvedic medicine and that a certain dose of its powder can cure jaundice, gall bladder, etc. The hindu as well as Buddhist drink water from a Shankha before they break a fast and almost all temple prayer are accompanied by the blowing of the Shankha.

CHAKRA

འཁོར་ལོ།

Tshonchhei Khorlo Chada khorlo

Chakra or the wheel that represents mystical power and absolute completeness is an emblem or to.be used as a holy symbol by Hindus and Buddhist. Vishnu the Hindu god of preservation always holds a charka to do away with demons and to protect his devotees and to make sure that Dharma (righteousness) dose not retrograde. Chakra is associated with Yoga and Tantric Meditation because it is located as a five element of nature in the human body.

73

GHANTA
नेब्रा
Dilbu

The sound of Ghanta (Sanskrit word of Bell) is Hindu philosophy symbolizes the Nata - Bharma (Seed - sound) origination from Brahma, the supreme being. The ringing of the bell always has been an integral part of prayers for most religious. We find bells in every temple and thus, it is important to every religion.

GADA
द्युग्'र्तो
Yugto

Gada is a mace or club which is usually used as a weapon for face to face battle. As a ritual pretense it is made of human bone, usually decorated with a skull at the top. This provides protection to whom carrying it. It symbolise the power of natural law and time, which destroy everything along on its path. As a club it is often represented as a pestle and symbolically linked with the lingam and staff. It is the symbol of Vishnu, Shakti, Kali, Ganesh and Kumar. It is an attribute of Durga, Devi and Bhairav.

TRISHUL
ङे'ग्बासुख्या
Chesum

Trishul, the trident, is most powerful divine weapon and it is an attribute of lord Shiva, Shakti (Durga) and Kali. The trident of Shiva is called Sulla which is regarded as a magic weapon and that drives demon away. The three spines of Trishul are the reminder of creation, preservation and destruction. It may also reflect the three qualities of goodness, passion darkness which are in all things in different proportions. The shaft symbolize the axis of the universe.

VEENA
ন্ম'ম্ভুথা
Gyumang

Veena is a stringed musical instrument. It is the favorite of goddess Saraswati who is the idol of knowledge and wisdom who plays the music of love and life on the Veena.

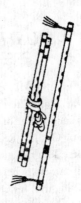

MURALI
ষ্ট্রীন্ন্নু'ইন্ন্না
Lingbu

Murali is a flute that is musical wind instrument of lord Krishna. Murali symbolize the inner desire and yearning for the highest.

DAMARU
ন্ন'ম'ন্তু
Damaru

Damru is a small double drum with leather thong tied in the middle of the drums. At the end is a peace of wood, bone or metal which makes sound when turned swiftly repeatedly upside down or side to side. Damru is made of two half skulls among the Tantrics which symbolize the primal sound, the origin of the phenomenal universe, also the rhythm, vibration and strength of the cosmos. It remains a part of stuff used in ritual worship along with the Ghanta and Shankha.

It is an attribute of Shiva (Natraja), the dancer and usually depicted along with the trident.

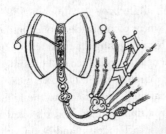

TORAN
ཕྱོ་འཕྲིལ།
Gokhim

Toran is a gateway Jading to the temple or a holy place for worship is semi circular in form and is played above the temple doorway. Toran are mostly found made on wood or stone and some are lavishly gilded with brass, others are even beautiful embellished with several artistic designs.

PUSHPA
མེ་ཏོག
Metog

Pushpa (Flowers) are offered to the god according to the season and the kind of flower chosen depends on the form of God, i.e. Red flower for ganesha or Durga goddess. Fragrance in the flowers creates a special environment where devotee is ready to continue a dialog with his God in his personal way.

DEEP
མཆོད་མེ།
Marmey

Deepa is a lamp where cotton wicks dipped in the purified ghee or butter. During the ritual festival or worship in the temple, deep lighted and presented to the God in the circular form. Devotee seeks a transition from darkness (ignorance) to the Light (knowledge). It is a ritual artefact and regarded a sacred symbol in both Hinduism and Buddhism.

DHOOP
བསངས།
Dugpoi

Dhoop is incense, that give beautiful fragrance and are used as an essential part of our daily Poojas. Dhoop represents the Gandh (fragrance) aspect of the senses. An everlasting sense of depicting a pure Gandha sense is the Dhoop. As ritual object, incense is burnt as an offering to deities, burning your desires is symbolized in this air purifying ritual.

NAIBEDHA *(Prasad)*
བྱིན་རླབས།
Jinlap

God is always content and is source of food. We offer food (mental food) to him in shape of our love and devotion to him. We receive all food by grace of God and therefore it is his food that we are blessed with. Food is sanctified and taken by devotees as 'PRASAD'.

THALI
སྡེར།
Derma

A copper Thali (plate) is used specially for placing the various Pooja items. The use of the copper plate is an intrinsic part of the daily traditional Pooja routine followed by Hindus all over the world. Therefore Thali is a most important item for daily customary Pooja and for any special festive occasions.

MALA
ཕྲེང་བ།
Thengwa

Males is a term of the mantra beads. It is a string of 108 beads, a number which has special meaning both among the Hindus and the Buddhists. The ordinary one is made of woods, bones, pearls or crystals. The best one is made of Tulashi woods, Rudraksha seeds both of them are regarded as a sacred ritual object. The males represents the never ending cycle or eternal cycle of time. Males is an attribute of Brahma, Krishna, Ganesh and Swaraswati.

TULASHI
ཚུལ་ཤི་མེ་ཏོག
Tulashi-sing

In Hinduism, Tulashi (Basil) is regarded as a holy plant and it is common all over Nepal and India. Almost every house of Hindu has this plant. It is also an herbal having wonderful healing power.

RUDRAKSHA
རུ་དྲཱ་ཀྴ
Raksha

Shiva Purana describes Rudrakshas origin as Lord Shiva's tears. He had been meditating for many years for the welfare of all creatures. On opening the eyes, hot drops of tears rolled down and the mother earth gave birth to Rudraksha trees.

The Rudraksha Beads have been worn by the Yogis for thousands of years for the Fearless Life on their Path to Enlightenment and Liberation.

78

CHANDANA *(Sandalwood)*

ཙན་དན།

Chandan

Lord Vishnu worshipers apply a Chandan Tilak of the shape of "U" and Lord Shiva worshipers applied a Tripundra Bhasma on their forehead. The chandan which is offered to the Lord is taken back as prasad and applied on foreheads. Chandan - made from sandal-paste, and placed as a Tilak or sacred mark on the forehead. This is a mark of auspiciousness, which is placed at the point where the third eye of wisdom or the spiritual eye is located. Chandan has a very cooling effect, and great medicinal value. Tilak is a blessing of the Lord and protection against wrong tendencies and forces.

Shiva Chandan - Devotees of Lord Shiva apply Chandan in 3 horizontal lines, using Bhasma or ashes.

Vaishnava Chandan - The Vaishnavites, or the devotees or Lord Vishnu, apply three vertical lines with sandal-paste.

Devi Chandan - Worshippers of Durga place the dot on their foreheads with the red Devi chandan.

KUSHA
རྩ་ཀུ་ཤ།

The Kusha Grass (Poacynosuroids) and Durva Grass (Agrostis linearis) are the holiest of all grasses. In all hindu rituals Kusha is must and when it is wounded round the finger, it makes the person fit to perform even the most solemn rites. The Durva grass is sacred to Ganesha and is offered to him during Pooja. Kusha grass is also offered in worship to many deities. Kusha grass is considered to be Vishnu, according to the Vishnu Purana. According to the story of Ramayana, Kusha is considered as hair of Goddess Sita.

GAUMATA (Cow)
བ་ཕྱུགས།
Ba-lang

The cow is sacred animal to the Hindus and she is respected as "Gaumata!" (cow, the Mother) and "Aditi" (mother of gods). The sacredness of the cow is a central and crucial element in Hindu belief. The cow is supposed to be the living symbol of Mother Earth.

For the early migrants the cow was an indispensable member of the family. As agriculture was the occupation of the migrants, the cow provided them with milk and its by-products and also necessities of life such as manure for the farm. It is believed that lord Krishna was cowherd and this animal was his favorite.

PUSTAKA (Book)
དཔེ་དེབ།
Leg-bam

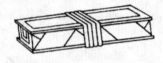

Among the Hindus the Pustak refers to the Vedic volumes, the storehouse of spiritual knowledge. Thus it is a symbol of mother lap, the lotus or the wisdom. It is an attribute of Brahma, Saraswati and Vishnu.

KALASH
བུམ་པ།
Bumba

This water jug believed to contain Amrit, the elixir of immortality. It represents wisdom and place on the altar as an important ritual artifact. This is an attribute of Goddess Laxmi.

KAMANDALU
ལྱུང་བཟེད།
Lungtse

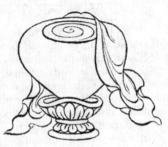

This water jug believed as a ritual artifact that is container into which the nectar is poured but it is also served to pour it out. Ascetics usually carried it with them. It is an attribute of Shiva, Brahma, Saraswati, Ganga and Varun.

RAKHI

Through the passage of time festivals are undergoing modifications. Raksha Bandhan is also known as Rakhi. Rakhi has become a sacred festival for sisters and brothers. Sisters tie this holy thread around the wrist of their brothers. Priests tie them to people of his congregation. The chaste bond of love between a brother and a sister is one of the deepest and noblest of human emotions.

PEEPAL TREE
(Ashvattha in Sanskrit)
 བྱང་ཆུབ་ཤིང་།
Jyang-chup-sing

Peepal tree is considered equivalent to Lord Vishnu and no Hindu dares to cut this tree, even if it comes in the way of doing any work. Its botanical name is Fichus religious. During the Vedic period, its wood was used to make fire by friction. The Peepal is used extensively in Ayurveda. Its bark yields the tannin used in to rearing leather. Its leaves when heated in ghee, are applied to cure wounds.

SHIKHA (Tupi)
དབུ་སྐྲའི་གཙུག་ཕུད།
Chugfu

This is a little tuft of hair on the shaven head of male Hindu. It is also known as Bodi. On unshaved head it is usually a little longer, it hangs out prominently. It sticks up in the center of the head and is regarded as sacred for it is the repository of spiritual energy. In Tantra it is considered the point where the spirit enters at the time of initiation and the departure or exit point at the time of death. It is protective symbol as it presence a Hindu can face any eventuality including death.

JANAI (Janahav)
སྐེ་ཐག
Tshanku

Janai is a sacred thread made with a yellow cotton string which is worn across the chest or tied around the wrist of the right hand especially by the Brahmans and Chettris. This thread is only given to males during a lengthy and impressive religious ceremony called the 'Bratabandhand. This cord initiates them into manhood and commands them to faithfully the follow the religion. It has 'three string' which is a symbol of body, speech and mind, and when the knots are tied the wearer is supposed to gain complete control over each.

BRAHMA

ལྷ་ཚངས་པ།

Lha-tshangpa

In Hinduism, Brahma represents the creative aspects, Vishnu the sustaining aspects and Shiva the destructive aspects. Brahma has arms that represent the four points of the compass. His formation has shown holding a vase of water, symbolizing the water from which the universe evolved, a rosary for counting the passage of time, a sacrificial spoon linking him with the Brahmin priests and their traditional told in the offering of sacrifices and the four Vedas, ancient sacred books of the Hindus.

He may be depicted on a lotus throne. He is often bearded, and may wear a black or white garment. In Hindu cosmology, the time of creation is recorded in the days and life of Brahma. When Brahma is awaken from his sleep and open his eyes, a universe and everything in it was created. When he shuts his eyes at the end of the day to go to sleep, that universe comes to the end. One day in the life of Brahma is known as KALPA, that is at last about 4,320 million human years.

VISHNU *Khyabjyuk*

ཁྱབ་འཇུག

Hindu God

Vishnu is the preserver of the universe and the upholder of the Dharma. It is believed that he has pervaded the universe by descending to earth in different forms when the forces of evil threaten to overcome the forces of good. According to the GEETA, whenever Lord Vishnu sees Dharma declining, the weak and innocent suffering, he comes down to the earth in different form of incarnation to undo the wrong. The different incarnation of Vishnu are known as Matsya (fish), Kurma (Tortoise), Varaha (Boar), Narsinmha (Half human, half lion) Vamana, Parasurama, Rama, Krishna, Buddha & Kalki.

SHIVA

ལྷ་དབང་ཕྱུག

Wangchug-chenpo

Shiva represents the power of destruction but as the old has to be destroyed to give rise to the new; he is also respected as the lord of creation. He has many synonyms as Maha-deva or Maha-Ishwor (great-god), Maha-yogi (great ascetic), Nata-raja (lord of the dance), Pashupati (lord of the animals), Neel-Kantha (blue-throated), Rudra and so on. His name means 'auspicious' or 'kindly' and this should be kept in mind in any interpretation of the symbols associated with him. His most characteristic weapon is the trident, a reminder of his role in the whole process of creation, preservation and destruction. It may also reflect the three qualities of goodness, passion and darkness which are in all things in different proportions.

Another typical feature on images of Shiva is his third eye which represents spiritual insight and the ability to burn up anything which may hinder such insight. The three horizontal lines on his forehead have been interpreted as representing the three sources of light - fire, sun and moon; or his ability to see the past, present and future. The snakes around his neck or across his body represent the evolutionary power within the human body, the spiritual power which may be developed through yoga and also Shiva!s power to deal with death. He is frequently depicted sitting on a tiger skin, the symbol of the cruel forces of nature, over which he is lord. Shiva vehicle is Nandi a white bull which represents strength and fertility. Shiva!s consort (wife or partner) is Parvati.

GANESH
ཚོགས་བདག
Tsokdak

Ganesh the god of wisdom, is the defender and remover of hindrance has to be worshipped at first before patronized any other gods. The image of Ganesh has an elephant's head and a large human body. The elephant's head symbolizes the gaining of knowledge through listening and reflection.

The two tusks one full and the other broken, reflect the existence of perfection and imperfection in the physical world. There is a wealth of symbolism associated with his pot belly. It has been interpreted as reflecting an ability to digest whatever experiences life brings. It may also be seen as a sign of well-being and of his role as provider of earthly riches. This reflects a balance between the practical and spiritual life.

LAKSHMI

ལྷ་མོ་ནོར་རྒྱུན་མ།

Norgyunma

Lakshmi, one of the forms of mother, is the goddess of fortune and wealth. She is among the most worshipped of all gods and goddess in Hinduism. She is associated with the most important festival among the multitude of Nepal & India, "Lakshmi-Puj a!' which takes place in the new moon night of November. Lakshmi puja is significant for those who believes, celebrating it will bring blessings and fortune for the coming year.

As goddess of good fortune she is depicted with four arms. Two of her hands hold lotus flowers and a third pours out wealth in the form of gold coins. Her fourth hand is held out in the gesture of blessing. But she is also the goddess of beauty and as such is shown as a young and beautiful goddess decorated with jewels and with only two arms.

PARVATI *(Shakti)*

ལྷ་མོ་ལྱུ་མ།

Umadevi

Parvati, daughter of the Himalayas, represents the gender qualities of the Mother Goddess. Her docile obedience to her husband, Shiva, is seen as a model of the worshipper's relationship to God. It should be noted, however, that behind Parvati lays the power of the Mother Goddess which is seen by many Hindus to be greater than that of the deities themselves.

Parvati is never seen without her husband Shiva, therefore, she is seen as the Sakti (energy, potency, consort, wife) of Shiva. It is believed that another formation of Parvati is Goddess Durga (Mother Shakti), and exists in various divine (both friendly and fearful) forms. Two of her fierce but very powerful forms are Durga (Goddess beyond reach) and Kali (Goddess of destruction). Parvati reflects the gentle aspects whereas Durga and even more so, the mysterious goddess Kali, reflect the fiercer elements. Ganesha, the god depicted with an elephant's head and a human body, is one of Shiva!s and Parvati s sons. Both have eight hands and great power and energy (shakti). Durga rides on a lion and Kali rides on a corpse of a demon. Parvati was called Sati in her previous divine incarnation.

SARASWATI

ལྷ་མོ་དབྱངས་ཅན་མ།

Lhamo Yangchenma

Saraswati is the goddess of wisdom and fine arts. She particularly attracts the worship of students. She is often represented dressed in white (sign of purity) and rides on a white goose (swan) or seated on a full blown lotus. Objects associated with Saraswati are the Veena (a stringed musical instrument), a flute, a rosary and a book. Sanskrit, the ancient sacred language of Hinduism, is said to have been created by her. A peacock is sitting next to Saraswati and is anxiously waiting to serve as her vehicle. A peacock depicts unpredictable behavior as its moods can be influenced by the changes in the weather. Saraswati is using a swan as a vehicle and not the peacock. This signifies that one should overcome fear, indecision, and fickleness in order to acquire true knowledge.

She has four hands representing four aspects of human personality in learning; mind, intellect, alertness and ego. The two front arms indicate her activity in the physical world and the two back arms signify her presence in the spiritual world. The four hands represent the four elements of the inner personality. The mind is represented by the front right hand, the intellect by the front left hand, the conditioned consciousness by the rear left hand, and the ego by the rear right hand.

DURGA

ལྷ་མོ་ཁྲོ་མོ།

Thromo

The worship of Goddess Durga is very popular among Hindus. She is also called by many other names, such as Parvati, Ambika, and Kali. In the form of Parvati, She is known as the divine spouse of Lord Shiva and is the mother of her two sons, Ganesha and Karttikeya, and daughter Jyoti.

The name Durga means 'inaccessible. The Sanskrit word Durga means a fort, or a place that is protected and thus difficult to reach. Though loving and kind to those who worship her, as the consort of Shiva in her warrior form, she symbolizes the violent and destructive qualities of the Mother Goddess (Shakti). Goddess Durga represents the power of the Supreme Being that preserves moral order and righteousness in the creation. She has eighteen arms, carrying many objects and she is wearing red clothes. The red color symbolizes action and the red clothes signify that she is always busy destroying evil and protecting mankind from pain and suffering caused by the evil force. The weapons which she holds includes Shivas trident, Vishnds discuss, a bow and arrow, a sword and shield, and a javelin are for the destruction of evil and the protection of good.

RAMA *(Rama, Sita and Laxman)*
དགའ་བྱེད།
Gajey

In Hinduism Lord Rama is worshipped as a seventh incarnation of Lord Vishnu. Rama is very popular among all Hindus, as is evident by the numerous temples dedicated to him in Nepal and India. In the temple and images, Rama is usually shown with his faithful wife Sita, devoted brother Lakshmana, and his beloved devotee Hanuman. The life story of Rama and the main purpose of his incarnation, to destroy the demon king Ravana, are described in the great epic Ramayana.

HANUMAN

ཧ་ནུ་མ་ན།

Hanuman

Hanuman, a great devotee of Lord Rama, is particularly associated with the Ramayana, the story of Rama and Sita.

In the story, Sita, Rama's wife, is kidnapped by the evil king, ten-headed demon Ravana who carries her off to his fortress in the island of Lanka. At great risk to his own safety, Hanuman finds Sita and then returns to help Rama build a bridge towards the island to rescue Sita.

During the ensuing battle, Rama!s brother Lakshmana was fatally wounded. Hanuman was sent to fetch healing herbs which grew on a particular mountain. Unable to identify the herbs, he uprooted the whole mountain and brought it back to the site of the battle thus saving Lakshmana's life. Images of Hanuman often show him holding the mountain in his hand. As a model for human devotion to God, he is often depicted with paws clasped together in reverence.

He is s symbol of strength and loyalty and represents the concept that animals are also a creation of God.

KRISHNA

ཀྲ་ཥྞ

Krishna

Lord Krishna is the eighth and the most popular manifestation of Lord Vishnu. It is believed that Krishna was born in Vrindavan of India, where he was brought up by the cowherd family of Yashoda and Nanda. His childhood playmates were gopas (cowherd boys) and gopis (cowherd girls), who were greatly devoted to him. The Gopis represents the individual souls trapped in physical bodies.

He is typically depicted with blue-black skin, wearing a yellow loin cloth and a crown of peacock feather. Lord Krishna is also shown with his pet cow, his childhood favorite. Lord Krishna performed many divine sports (leela) as a child. He is also shown with his childhood devotee Radha who was his favorite gopi or cow girl. The Hindu tradition is rich in poetry about the love of Krishna and Radha which is valued both as an expression of human love but also as being symbolic of the love of the soul for God. The Lord is usually remembered and worshipped as Radha-Krishna.

93

KUMAR KARTIKEYA

གཤེན་རྨུ།

Kumar Kartekiya

Kumar Kartikeya, is the god of war. There are several strange stories told regarding Karttikeyis birth. He is the son of either Agni or Shiva. In Vedic times, he was the son of Agni and the river Ganges, but he was conceived in an odd way. In another, later story, it is said that Karttikeya is the son of Shiva and Parvati.

Kartikeya has several names. As he was breast-fed by six Karittika deities, he is called 'Kartikeya: He has six faces so he is 'Shanmulcha!. Because of his omniscience, he is 'Subrahmanya:. He is the leader of the divine armies so he is called 'Mahasena: He is also known as Skanda, Kumar, Shikhivahana, Guha, and so on.

He also seems to be the god of male virility. He is usually depicted as a youthful man full of vigor who has six heads. Sometimes he has twelve arms and twelve legs. He represents a person of perfection. While Ganesh removes all obstacles, Skanda bestows all spiritual power of knowledge.

INDRA
བརྒྱ་བྱིན།
Gyajin

Indra is the God of firmament and the king of the abode of Gods. In the early Vedic age, Indra is the top ranking figure among Gods. Yet, he is not equivalent to Omakar or Brahma because he has a parentage.

His complexion is golden and sparkling; he rides on golden chariot drawn by two red strong horses with a thick and flowing manes and pointed tails. His favorite weapon is the thunderbolt which he carries in his right hand; sometimes he is also represented as having a big bow with long pointed arrows as well as hook and a net. He is the ruler of the atmosphere and weathers are at his command.

VISWOKARMA

ལས་སྦུ་ཚོགས།

Vishowkarma

According to Rig Veda, Vishwa Karma is the divine architect of the whole universe. He is the personification of the creative power that welds heaven and earth together. He is the son of Brahma.

He is painted white, has a club in his right hand, wears a crown, a necklace of gold, rings on his wrists and holds tools in his left hand. He is the revealer of Sthapatya Veda, or the science of mechanics and architecture. Mahabharat describes him as "The Lord of the arts, executor or a thousand handicrafts, the carpenter of the Gods, the most eminent of artisans, the fashioner of all the ornaments, on whose craft all menu subsist, and whom, a great and immortal god, they continually worship."

He is the presiding deity of all the craftsmen and architects.

AGNI
མེ་ལྷ།
Me-lha

Agni Deva (Fire God) has been worshipped by Hindus from the Vedic ages till today. Agni is one of the three supreme deities of the Rig Veda, viz., Agni, Vayu and Surya. These three Gods preside over earth, air and sky respectively.

In Rig Veda, largest number of hymns are addressed to Agni. Agni is the son of Angiras and the grandson of Sandila, one of the seven great sages. Vishnu Puran, however, claims that Agni is the eldest son of Brahma. His wife is Swaha and through his marriage he has three sons, Pavak, Pavman and Suchi.

VAYU-DEVA

ཀླུང་ལྷ།

Loonglha

Vayu is the God of the air. Vayu is the wind who stirs the clouds, the blow, the breath of the world of the devas and of all the breathing but he is also beings. Vayu is a fierce god. He drives his horses furiously, sometimes a thousand of them. He is thought of as the god of rapid motion and therefore the father of the fleet-footed. As with the other gods Vayu can be prayed to for help. In the epic of Hinduism, Vayu is described as a father of Hanuman, who could move with the speed of air, and of Bhima, who was called the swift.

VARUN

ཆུ་ལྷ།

Chhyu Lha

Varuna is the god of oceans and he is guardian of the west. In pre-Vedic times, he was the supreme lord of the cosmos, the keeper of divine order, the bringer of rain. In Vedic times, the worship of Varuna fell off as he was supplanted by Indra as king of the gods. He is shown as a fair complexioned man riding a monster fish called MAKARA. He may have two or four hands and in one of his right hands he carries a noose.

SURYA-DEVA

ཉི་མའི་ལྷ།

Nyima

Surya, the Sun, a living god, everyone see, perceive and pray. Though he is visible, he also has been presented in a variety of forms. He is the life-giver and time-giver. In the six sects established by Adi Sankara, Souram is one devoted to Sun God. Even in other religious, Sun worship has place. In the Zodiac, Sun occupies a prominent place in the Centre.

The griha is the source of life and he is therefore described as the life-giver (Pranadhata). He helps one gain his eyesight and Suryanamaskar (worship by prostration) will strengthen one's bones, cure illness, however sever it may be, cleanses the devotee from his sins and bestrows on him progeny, wealth, good-health and long life. He is the cause for rain-fall benefiting the world.

CHANDRA DEVA

ཟླ་བའི་ལྷ།

Dawa

Chandra (the Moon) is loving god. Pleasing to children as well as elders universally appealing to everyone whatever my be the religion of the onlooker. Sages and devotees invoke the Goddess mother in Chandra and meditate for hours.

Moon cause's nightfall strengthens the mind, purifies the blood and is considered as the mother who radiates nectar (Amrut). Worship of Chandra is said to be beneficial for relief from all sorrows, helps in curing mental afflictions, etc. His cool rays radiate happiness around. He adores the head of Lord Siva. Worshipping Chandra on Monday is said to be very effective in getting one's prayers answered.

In the Zodiac he is the lord of Cancer. He stays 2 1/4 days in each Rasi completing a round of the 12 Rasis in 27 days.

YAMA

Sinje

Yam (Yams) is the God of death who judges and punishes souls and is the lord of infernal regions one visits after the cessation of life.

He is represented as of a green colour, four-armed, clad in garments of fire, crowned and seated on a buffalo. He holds a mace and noose, and drags the souls of the condemned out of the bodies to the judgment-seat.

He is the embodiment of the rule of law and imparts justice according to deeds. The word "Yam' means the restrainer' it is he who keeps the mankind in check.

KUBERA

ནོར་ལྷུ་ཛེ་བྲལ།

Jambala

Kubera, the god of wealth, is also "own as Dhanapati, "Lord of riches". He is the guardian of the north and is associated with all the treasures of the earth that lie underground. His white body is dwarfish, has three legs and eight teeth. He has two to four hands and may carry in his hands a mace, a purse containing money, a vase, a fruit and a bowl and two hands in the boon giving and protective modes. If shown as having two hands he will carry a bowl and a money bag.

His body is covered with jewels and other ornaments. For moving around he has a chariot called Pushpak. He is also called the gods of Yaksas.

SOME OF RITUAL OBJECT
HOLDING GESTURES
ཕྱག་རྒྱ།

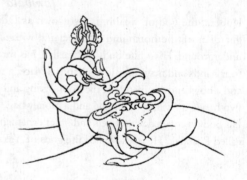

HAND GESTURES
(MUDRA)
ཕྱག་རྒྱ།

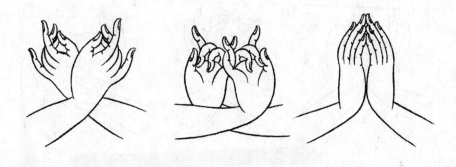

HAND GESTURES
(MUDRA)
ཕྱག་རྒྱ།

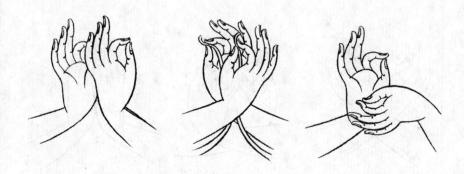

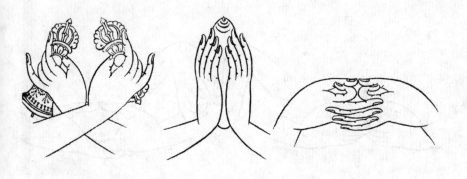

HAND GESTURES
(MUDRA)
ধুন্নক্রা

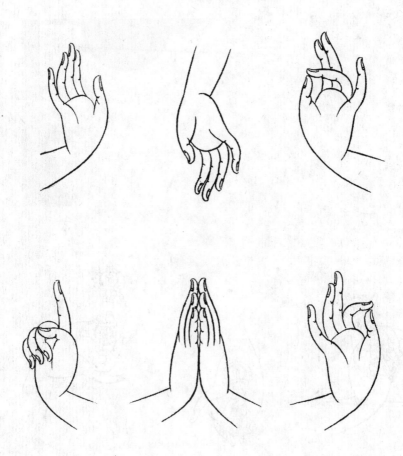

HAND GESTURES
(MUDRA)
ཕྱག་རྒྱ།

HAND GESTURES
(MUDRA)
ཕྱག་རྒྱ།

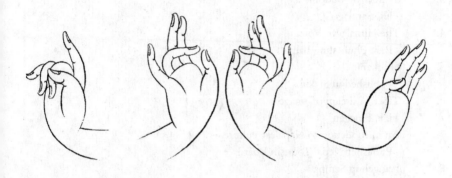

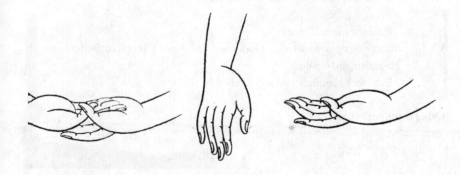

Bibliography

1. An encylopedia of Tibetan Symbol & Motifs
    - Robert Beer
2. An iconography of Buddhism and Hinduism
    - Eva Rudy Jansen
3. Symbol of Buddhism
    - J.R. Santiago
4. The Himalayan Voice
    - Pun. Phuntshng Lama
5. Hunkara
    - Published in Sikkim
6. Tibet, A dream of image
    - J. F. Finegan
7. An introduction to Nepalese culture
    - Publisher Nepal Tourism Board
8. Jyangchup Sempa
    - Lama P. Pakhrin
9. Cultural attraction in Nepal
    - Publisher Nepal Tourism Board
10. Biography of Legends of Tibet
    - A Tibetan booklet published from India
11. Karmapa paper
    - Published from France
12. Short description of Gods, Goddesses and Ritual Objects of Buddhism and
    Hinduism in Nepal
    - Publisher Handicraft Association of Nepal (HAN)

Other many periodicals.